More Spanish for Little Boys

A Spanish workbook for little boys

Written and Illustrated by: Yvonne Crawford

www.languageforlittlelearners.com

About this workbook

This book is a continuation of Spanish for Little Boys. In this second level your son will continue his exploration of the Spanish language while engaging in activities that will help to motivate him. He will design his own monster, make his own spaceship, open a sweet shop and much, much more.

This workbook is created especially for parents who do not have any prior knowledge of Spanish. You and your son can embark on a journey of learning a foreign language together. Everything you need is inside this workbook, including a pronunciation guide, dictionary and teaching hints.

Every lesson will consist of a list of vocabulary words with pictures, three activities your son can do in the workbook with your guidance and two activities you can do together without the workbook for further practice. Each new word that is introduced will have its pronunciation next to it.

In the appendices there is a learning slide that he can color after he completes each lesson. This will help your child to see, and take pride in his progress.

Try not to put stress on your son to have perfect pronunciation or to remember every single word. If he forgets a word, simply repeat it and then use it in a sentence a few times; eventually he will catch on. It is important for him (and you) to have a positive first experience with learning a foreign language. It will encourage him to continue and succeed in the future with more language studies.

Table of Contents

Lección 1

Ocean Creatures

Vocabulary:

la ballena *lah-bah-**yay**-nah*
whale

el pulpo *ehl-**pool**-poh*
octopus

la estrella de mar
*lah-ehs-**tray**-yah-day-mahr*
starfish

el tiburón *ehl-tee-boo-**rohn***
shark

el cangrejo *ehl-kan-**gray**-hoh*
crab

Fun Phrases:

sí	*see*	yes
no	*noh*	no
quizás	*kee-**sahs***	maybe

Teaching Tips:

- Throughout the day, ask your children questions in either Spanish or English and then prompt them to answer you in Spanish with the words they learned above for yes, no and maybe.

- If your child asks you what a word is in Spanish that is not listed in this book, look it up in a Spanish/English dictionary or on a website and then create a little dictionary for them out of a small spiral notebook. You can even have them draw the picture in order to help them to remember the word.

Actividad Uno

¡*Hola!* My name is Ramón. It's nice to meet you. Can you match the picture of each ocean creature to its correct name in Spanish?

la ballena

el pulpo   la estrella de mar

Actividad Dos

Now you can greet each of my ocean friends in Spanish! For each picture above greet the animal, by sayimg '¡*Hola!*', then say the name of the animal.

Actividad Tres

Tell me which of these animals you like. If you like them write *sí*, and if you don't like them write *no*.

Me gusta... I like...

_____

_____

_____

_____

_____

_____

Actividad Cuatro

Your Very Own Aquarium

What you will need:

construction paper
crayons and/or markers
glitter
glue stick
scissors

What to do:

1. Draw a big aquarium on blue construction paper.
2. Draw ocean animals (or cut them out from magazines) and glue to the aquarium.
3. Use crayons, markers and glitter to decorate the fish. Practice your colors in Spanish as you color them.
4. Hang the finished aquarium on the fridge and every time you go to the fridge, point to the animals and say their names in Spanish.

Actividad Cinco

Starfish Toss

What you will need:

construction paper
scissors
pencil
cardboard
cap or cup

What to do:

1. Draw and cut out 10 starfish. You can trace the one from the workbook if you would like.
2. Glue them to pieces of cardboard.
3. Get your mother or father to help you cut them out.
4. Toss the starfish into the cap or cup and count them in Spanish as you do: *una estrella de mar, dos estrellas de mar,* etc.

Lección 2
Creepy Monster Faces

Vocabulary:

el pelo *ehl-pay-loh*
hair

la cara *lah-kah-rah*
face

el ojo *ehl-oh-ho*
eye

la oreja *lah-oh-ray-hah*
ear

la nariz *lah-nah-rees*
nose

la boca *lah-boh-kah*
mouth

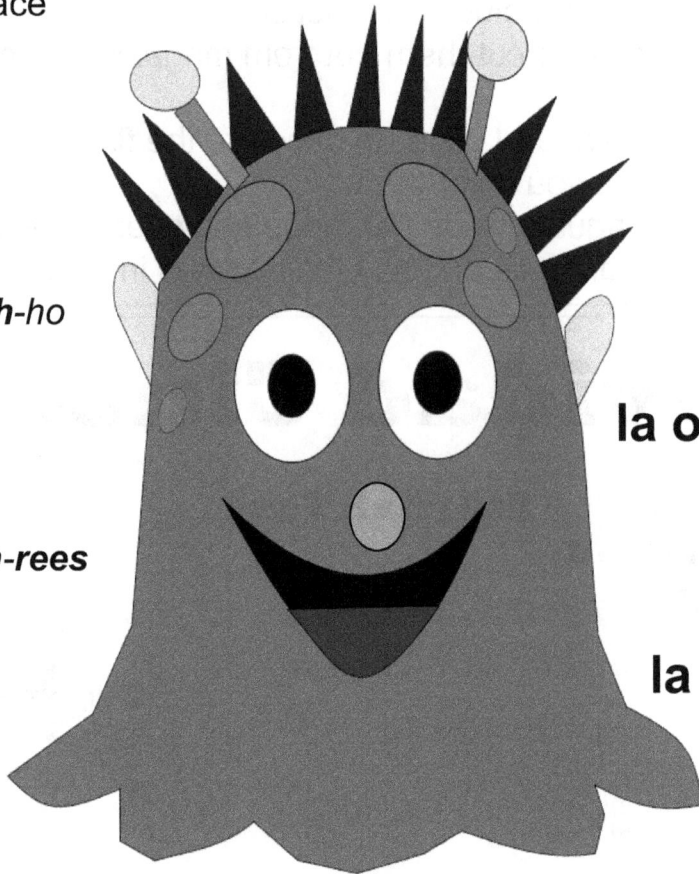

Fun Phrases:

tengo miedo	**tayn**-goh-mee-**ay**-doh	I'm scared
tienes miedo	tee-**ehn**-ehs-mee-**ay**-doh	you're scared
no tengo miedo	noh-**tayn**-goh-mee-**ay**-doh	I'm not scared
no tienes miedo	noh-tee-**ehn**-ehs-mee-**ay**-doh	you're not scared
muy	**moo**-ee	very

Teaching Tips:

- Go through the lessons as fast or as slow as your child wants to go. Look to him for signs of fatigue. There is always tomorrow where you can take up where you left off today.

- Feel free to go back to the first book of Spanish for Little Boys in case your son has forgotten things like colors or numbers in Spanish. It's a good idea to go back and review earlier topics

Actividad Uno

Come and meet my monster friends. Each of them is missing one part of their faces. Say the name of the facial part that is missing in Spanish and then draw the missing parts on their face.

Actividad Dos

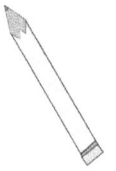

Oh no, one of my monster friends had to go away on vacation and he was supposed to spend the day with me. Can you draw me a monster friend? As you draw the different body and facial parts, say their names in Spanish. Make sure to use colors and say their names in Spanish too. Make the monster as scary as you want.

Actividad Tres

This is Ramón's favorite story about his adventure with a monster. Your mom or dad can read the story to you, and whenever you see a picture in the story, say the word in Spanish.

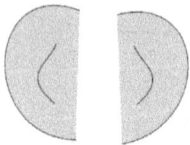

orejas

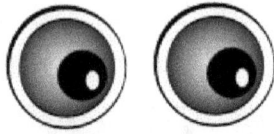

ojos

pelo

boca

nariz

monstruo

One day I was walking though the forest with my friend Pedro. I looked into the dark. I saw a   . However, I couldn't make out exactly what the   looked liked. I walked up closer to the   and I saw something that looked like huge light blue   . Looking even closer at him, I saw 2 round   . The   even had some purple spiky   . Who would've thought that a little creature like this would actually have some   . I even noticed that he had a rather round, orange   .

"Pedro?" I asked, "What do you think about this   ? Do you think that he is a good or bad?

"It's really hard to say," Pedro said. "Can you see his ?"

"I think I can see his . He's smiling," Ramón said.

"I have a flashlight, let's check him out to be sure," Pedro said.

Pedro pulled out a flashlight from his backpack and shined it on the monster. Both boys fell on the ground laughing. It wasn't a . It was Ramón's pet dog.

"Come here boy," Ramón said, "You really had me going!"

"We really need to be careful about our imaginations getting the best of us!" Pedro said.

"Yeah, that sure was some ," Ramón said, "Let's go home!"

Challenge:

- Help your child create their own monster story. They can describe the facial features to you in Spanish.

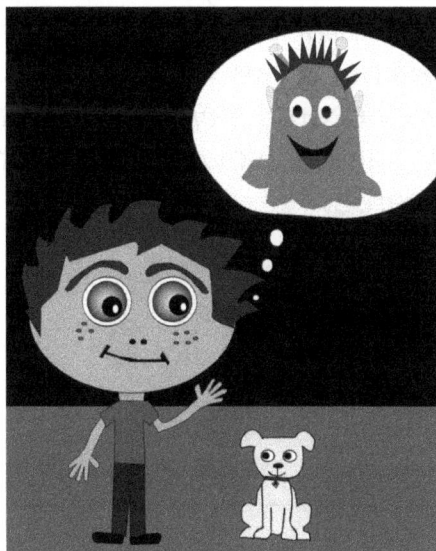

Actividad Cuatro

Yes, No, or Maybe?

Throughout the day, use your Spanish whenever you can! When your mom or dad asks you a question, say the answer in Spanish. Use: *sí, no,* or *quizás*. Every time you say one of these words today, you can come back to this workbook and record it on this page. Color a star each time you use one of your new Spanish words.

sí   **no**   **quizás**

☆ ☆ ☆ ☆ ☆ ☆ ☆ ☆ ☆

Actividad Cinco

Different Faces

What you will need:
your mom, dad or older sibling

What to do:
1. Your mom or dad will make a face.
2. In Spanish describe how it makes you feel. Is it a scary face? Is it not a scary face? If the face your parent makes is scary say: *Tengo miedo*. If the face does not make you scared, say: *No tengo miedo*. If the face makes you very scared say: *Tengo muy miedo*.
3. Switch roles with your parent. Now, it is your turn to try to make scary faces to make them scared.

Lección 3

Out of this World Numbers

Vocabulary:

el extraterrestre
*ehl-ex-trah-ter-**res**-tray*
alien

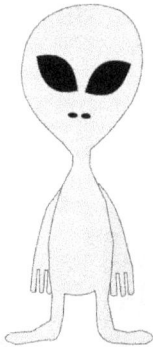

la astronave
*lah-as-troh-**nah**-vay*
spaceship

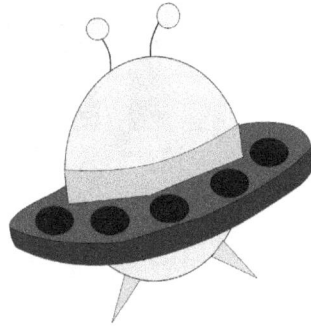

el planeta *ehl-plah-**nay**-tah*
planet

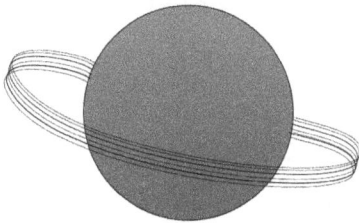

la luna *lah-**loo**-nah*
moon

la estrella
*lah-ehs-**tray**-yah*
star

la cometa *lah-koh-**may**-tah*
comet

11

once *ohn*-say
eleven

12

doce *doh*-say
twelve

13

trece *tray-say*
thirteen

14

catorce *kah-**tohr**-say*
fourteen

15

quince *keen-say*
fifteen

Teaching Tips:

- It's easy for children to learn numbers in order. It is much more difficult for them to be able to say them out-of-order. Make sure you help your son practice their numbers both ways.

Actividad Uno

Count the different objects in Spanish, then write the number in the box.

Actividad Dos

Color the picture according the codes at the bottom of the page.

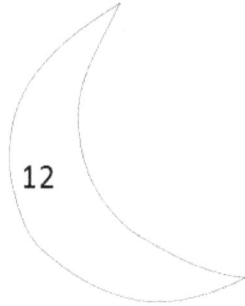

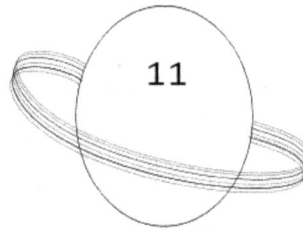

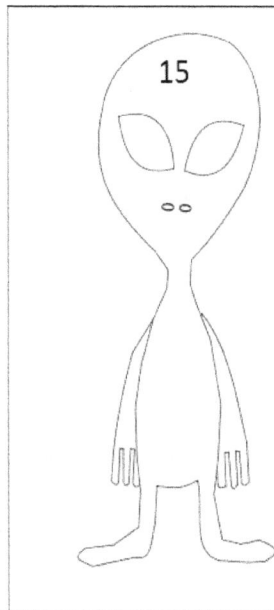

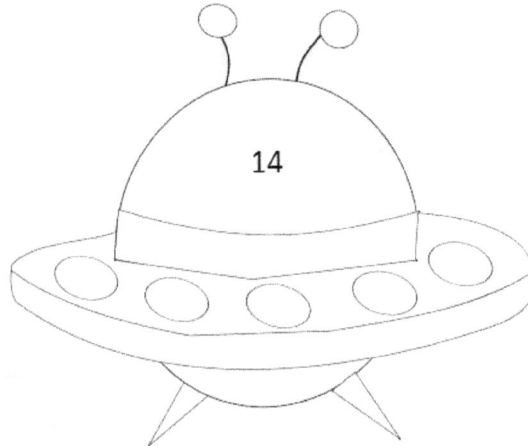

11

12

13

15

14

color key	
once - azul	catorce - negro
doce - verde	quince - rojo
trece - anaranjado	

Actividad Tres

Match the number to the word in Spanish. Then, write Spanish number in the space provided.

15

13

11

12

14

| doce | _ _ _ _ _ _ |

| catorce | _ _ _ _ _ _ |

| trece | _ _ _ _ _ _ |

| quince | _ _ _ _ _ _ |

| once | _ _ _ _ _ _ |

Actividad Cuatro

Counting in Twos and Fives

Practice your Spanish number by counting by twos, and fives. By doing this, you'll be able to remember all of the number more quickly. You can practice by counting your toys and grouping them first into sets of twos or fives. Have fun!

Actividad Cinco

Make You Own Spaceship

What you will need:
an empty toilet paper roll
tin foil
construction paper or streamers
scissors
glue

What to do:
1. Wrap the empty toilet paper roll with tin foil, leaving a little extra on one side.
2. Twist the extra foil to make the point of the space ship.
3. Add streamers or strips of construction paper to the other side to be the fire of the spaceship.
4. Launch your space ship by counting down the numbers in Spanish.

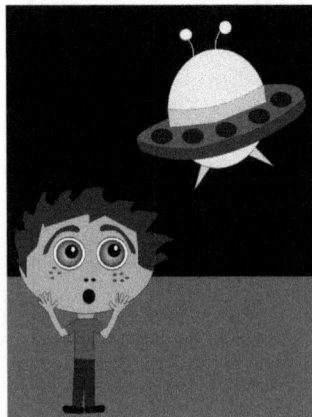

Lección 4

Polite Pirates

Vocabulary:

el barco pirata
*ehl-**bar**-koh-pee-**rah**-tah*
pirate ship

el mapa del tesoro
*ehl-**mah**-pah-del-tay-**soh**-roh*
treasure map

el sombrero
*ehl-sohm-**bray**-roh*
hat

el pirata *ehl-pee-**rah**-tah*
pirate

el cofre del tesoro
*ehl-**koh**-fray-del-tay-**soh**-roh*
treasure chest

la espada
*lah-ehs-**pah**-dah*
sword

Fun Phrases:

¡mucho gusto!	**moo**-choh-**goo**-stoh	nice to meet you
perdón	pehr-**dohn**	excuse me
¡buen apetito!	booehn-ah-pay-**tee**-toh	have a good meal
¡salud!	sah-**lood**	bless you (said after a sneeze)

Actividad Uno

Look at the pictures below. Draw a line from each picture to the correct phrase in Spanish.

¡salud!

¡mucho gusto!

¡buen apetito!

26

Actividad Dos

Look for the treasure chest at the end of this maze. As you pass each person on the maze, make sure you say *perdón,* to be polite.

Actividad Tres

Look at each picture below. Draw a line under your favorite pirate item and say the name in Spanish. Next, draw a *rojo* circle around your least favorite pirate item and say the name in Spanish. Finally, draw an *azul* circle around your mother's or father's favorite pirate item and say its name in Spanish.

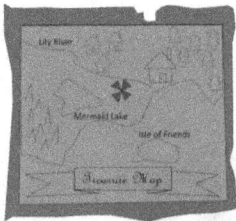

Actividad Cuatro

Arrrghhh I'm a Pirate

Dress up as a pirate and practice all of your favorite polite Spanish phrases as a pirate. Say things like *"Arrrgggghhh, ¡buen apetito!"* before your afternoon snack. Be creative, if you don't have a pirate costume, use a bandana or a towel and tie it on your head like a pirate!!

Have fun with this activity matey!

Actividad Cinco

Pirate and Space Bingo

What you will need:
the bingo cards and calling cards from the appendix of this book
markers for the bingo cards - penny or small stone
a hat or cap

What to do:
1. Your mother or father can cut the calling cards from the back of the book and put inside a hat.
2. One by one they will draw one piece of paper from the hat and say the name in Spanish.
3. Each time you hear a word, you look at your bingo card and try to find the picture. Place a marker on the spot if you have a match.
4. When you get 5 in a row, you win and you can shout out "BINGO!"
5. Try playing with a friend or a sibling and see who can win first!

BINGO!!!!!

Lección 5
Circus Fun

Vocabulary:

el circo
*ehl-**seer**-koh*
circus

el domador de leones
*ehl-doh-mah-**dohr**-day-lee-**ohn**-ays*
lion tamer

el payaso
*ehl-pah-**yah**-soh*
clown

el director de circo
*ehl-dee-rehk-**tohr**-day-**seer**-koh*
ringmaster

el funambulista
*ehl-foon-ah-boo-**lee**-stah*
tight-rope walker

dieciséis
*dee-ay-see-**says***
sixteen
16

diecisiete
*dee-ay-see-see-**ay**-tay*
seventeen
17

dieciocho
*dee-ay-see-**oh**-choh*
eighteen
18

diecinueve
*dee-ay-see-noo-**ay**-vay*
nineteen
19

veinte
vayin-tay
twenty
20

Actividad Uno

¡Hola! Look at the picture below. How many of my clown friends can you find? Try to find 12. As you find each one, circle it in *rojo* and count each one in Spanish.

Actividad Dos

Use your crayon and connect all of the dots to finish his picture. As you connect the dots say each number in Spanish!

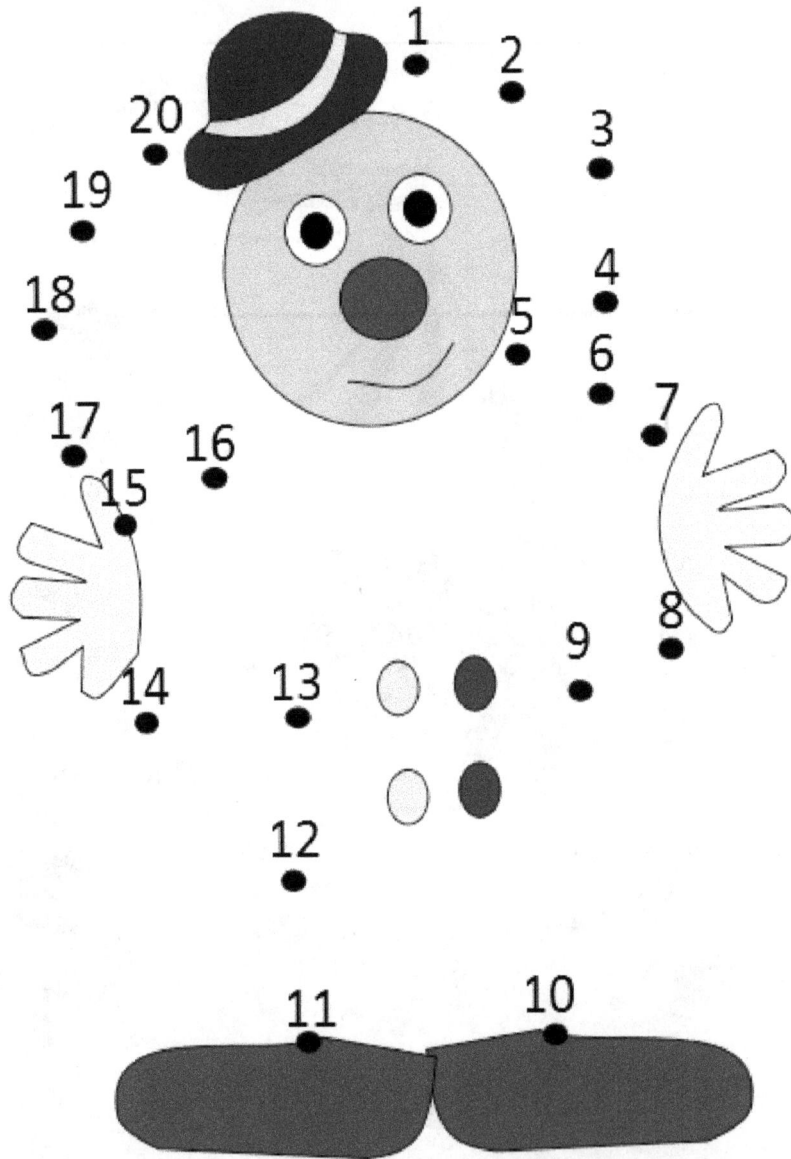

1
2
20
3
19
4
18
5
6
17   16
7
15
8
14   13   9
12
11   10

Actividad Tres

Count the pictures below in Spanish, and then circle the correct number.

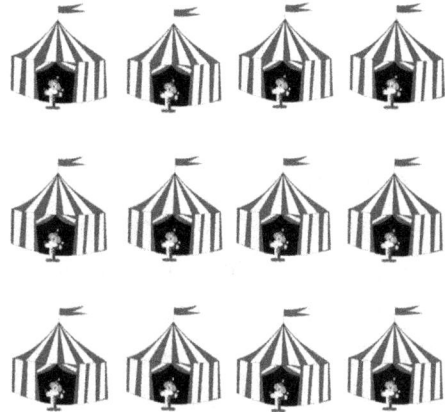

| 20 | 19 | 18 |

| 15 | 14 | 12 |

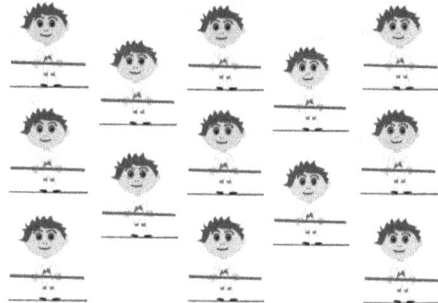

| 12 | 11 | 13 |

| 12 | 13 | 11 |

Challenge:

Start a collection of objects! Brainstorm with your parent about different things that could be in your collection (toy cars, rocks, sea shells, pencils, stamps, postcards). After gathering the objects for your collection, count the number of items in your collection in Spanish. Try to find at least 20 things for your collection.

Actividad Cuatro

A Life-size Clown

What you will need:

freezer paper
pencil
markers or crayons
scissors

What to do:

1. Roll out enough freezer paper and lay on it.
2. Have your mother or father draw an outline of you.
3. Now comes the fun part, turn yourself into a clown on the paper!
4. Draw and color clown clothes. Add big dots to the clothes and every time you draw one, count the dot in Spanish. Try to draw at least 20 big dots on your paper clown.

Actividad Cinco

A Dice Game

What you will need:

dice (3 or 4)
paper
pencil

What to do:

1. Roll the dice and count in Spanish how many dots you have.
2. Let the next person roll the dice and then they will count how many dots they have in Spanish. The person who has the most wins that round
3. Write down on the piece of paper who won that round and keep playing until one person wins ten games.

Challenge:

Learn to count higher in Spanish and play the game with 4 dice.

21– veintiuno   22 - veintidós   23 - veintitrés   24 - veinticuatro

Lección 6

Sports Time

Vocabulary:

el fútbol
*ehl-**foot**-ball*
soccer

el ciclismo
*ehl-see-**klees**-moh*
cycling

la natación
*lah-nah-tah-see-**ohn***
swimming

el baloncesto
*ehl-bah-lohn-**sehs**-toh*
basketball

el golf *ehl-gohlf*
golf

el hockey sobre hielo
*ehl-**hoh**-kayee-**soh**-bray-ee-ay-loh*
ice hockey

Fun Phrases:

juego	*hoo-**ay**-goh*	I play
juegas	*hoo-**ay**-gahs*	you play

Teaching Tips:

- When you say you play a sport in Spanish, you usually need to put '*al*' in front of the sport's name.
- Please note that *a + el = al*
- Here are some example sentences:

    Juego al baloncesto. - I play basketball.
    Juegas al fútbol. - You play soccer.

Actividad Uno

Draw a line from the picture of the sport, to the name of the sport in Spanish.

| el baloncesto |

| el golf |

| el hockey sobre hielo |

| la natación |

| el ciclismo |

Actividad Dos

Circle the six differences between the two pictures. As you find each difference count the number in Spanish.

Actividad Tres

Answer the questions below about the sports that you play. Circle *sí* for yes and *no* for no.

---

1. Do you like to play "*baloncesto*"?   *sí*   *no*

2. Have you ever played "*hockey sobre hielo*"?   *sí*   *no*

3. Do you like to "*ciclismo*"?   *sí*   *no*

4. Do you "*golf*" with your father?   *sí*   *no*

Now, draw a picture of your favorite sport. If you know its name in Spanish, write the name of the sport on the line below the picture frame.

Actividad Cuatro

Which Sport?

What you will need:

a basketball
a baseball
a soccer ball
bag

What to do:

1. Put all of the balls into the bag.
2. Pull out one ball and name the sport in Spanish.
3. Repeat until you finish saying the names of the sports for each ball.

Challenge:

Add equipment from other sports and add it to your bag. Instead of looking at the objects, try to guess what the sport is by simply touching the object before you take it out of the bag.

Actividad Cinco

Basketball Numbers

What you will need:

ten small balls
paper
tape
scissors
two hats or caps

13

What to do:

1. Cut out ten small pieces of paper and write one number on each piece of paper (11 to 20).
2. Tape one piece of paper to each ball.
3. Put all of the balls in one hat and put the other hat across the room.
4. Pull out one ball at a time and say the number in Spanish, then throw it into the other hat. If you make it, you score a point. Good Luck!

Lección 7

Sweet Shop

Vocabulary:

el algodón dulce
*ehl-ahl-goh-**dohn**-**dool**-say*
cotton candy

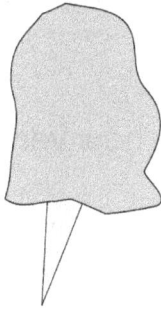

los dulces *lohs-**dool**-says*
candy

el pastel *ehl-pahs-**tehl***
cake

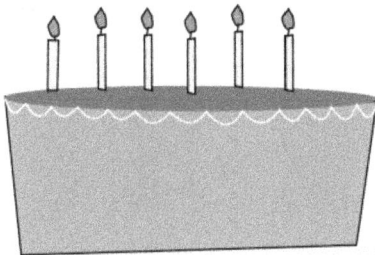

el pirulí *ehl-pee-roo-**lee***
lollypop

la galleta
*lah-gah-**yeh**-tah*
cookie

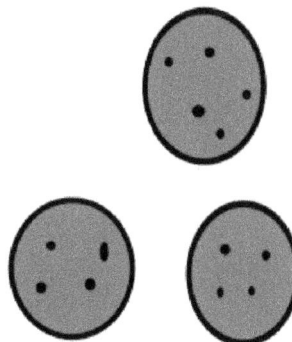

el refresco
*ehl-ray-**frehs**-koh*
soda pop

41

Fun Phrases:

como	**koh**-moh	I eat
comes	**koh**-mehs	you eat
bebo	**bay**-boh	I drink
bebes	**bay**-behs	you drink
quiero	kee-**eh**-roh	I want
quieres	kee-**eh**-rehs	you want

Challenge:

- You can help your children form questions using the new verbs listed above:

    ¿Qué quieres comer? - What do you want to eat?

    ¿Qué quieres beber? - What do you want to drink?

- Remember to teach these lessons as slowly or as quickly as your child needs. If your child is not ready for this challenge, you can always come back to it at a later time.

Actividad Uno

Look at all of the different *dulces* there are to eat. Circle the *dulce* that you think would taste the best. Then color all of the *dulces* according to the color key below.

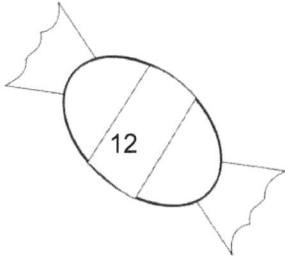

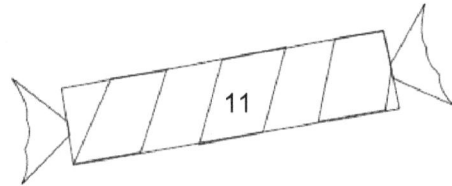

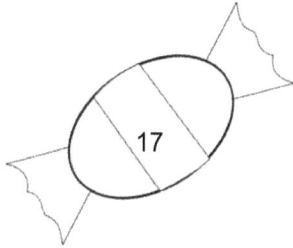

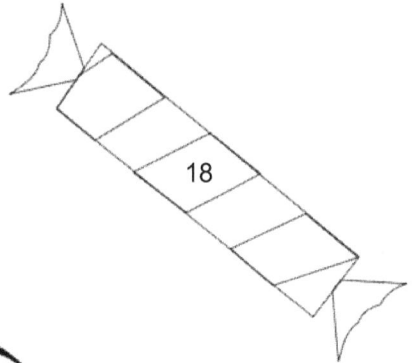

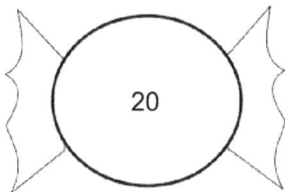

12

11

17

18

20

13

15

16

doce	rojo	once	negro
diecisiete	blanco	dieciocho	azul
trece	verde	quince	anaranja-do
dieciséis	negro	veinte	rojo

Actividad Dos

Answer the questions by drawing a picture in the box below each question
or circling the answer. (*qué*=what; *cuál*=which)

1. *¿Qué quieres comer?*

2. *¿Qué quieres beber?*

3. *Quieres un dulce?*   *sí*   *no*

4. *Cuál dulce?*

Actividad Tres

I need help filling these jars with *dulces*. Draw the amount of *dulces* listed under each jar. Thanks so much for helping me!

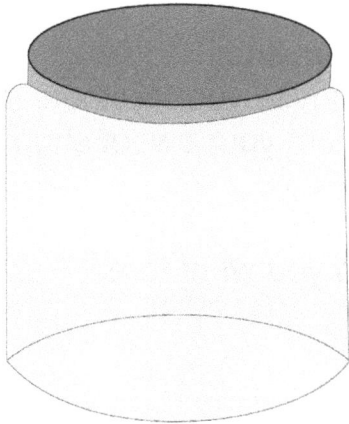

20

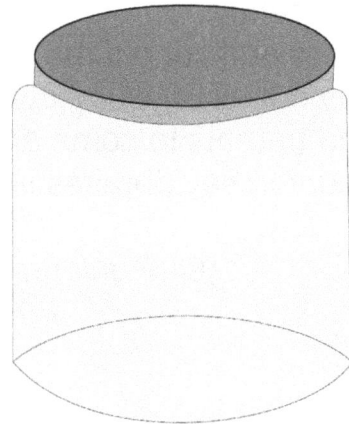

17

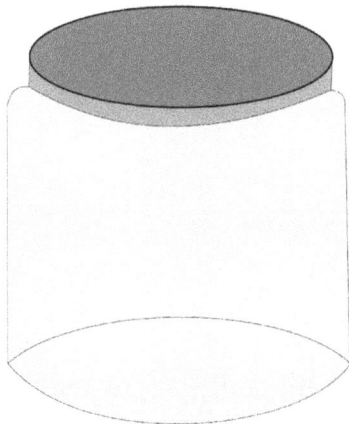

15

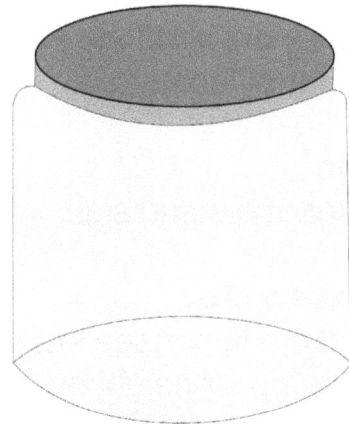

18

Actividad Cuatro

Your Own Sweet Shop

What you will need:

pictures of candy and sweets or blank paper
colors
scissors

What to do:

1. Either cut out from a magazine or draw your own pictures of sweets and candy.
2. Color and cut out the pictures that you've drawn.
3. Lay out all of your pictures on a table and invite your brothers, sisters and parents to come and pick out candy from your sweet shop.
4. You can say phrases like:

¿Qué quieres comer? - What do you want to eat?

Actividad Cinco

Lemonade Stand

What you will need:

a pitcher of lemonade
cups
a table
a lemonade stand sign

What to do:

1. Make a lemonade stand in your front yard.
2. Teach your neighbors a little Spanish. Use all of the Spanish you've learned so far. Say things like:

¡Hola! - Hello
¿Qué quieres beber? - What do you want to drink?

Lección 8
A Day at the Beach

Vocabulary:

la playa
*lah-**plah**-yah*
beach

la pelota de playa
*lah-pay-**loh**-tah-day-**plah**-yah*
beach ball

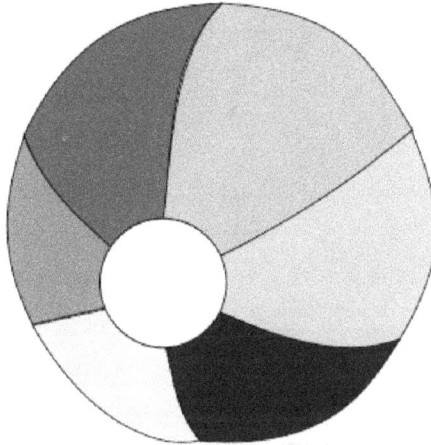

el mar
ehl-mahr
sea

la concha
*lah-**kohn**-chah*
shell

las gafas de sol
*lahs-**gah**-fahs-day-sohl*
sunglasses

la arena
*lah-ah-**ray**-nah*
sand

el castillo de arena
ehl-kah-**stee**-yoh-day-ah-**ray**-nah
sandcastle

Fun Phrases:

nado	*nah*-doh	I swim
nadas	*nah*-dahs	you swim

Teaching Tips:

- As your child learns new Spanish vocabulary, try to have them remember the article with the noun.

  el - masculine or *la* - feminine

Actividad Uno

Come join me at the beach! Look at the picture and point to objects and say their name in Spanish. Every time you say a name in Spanish, then color the object.

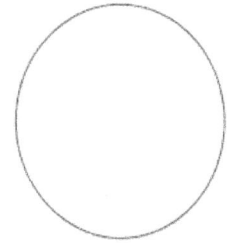

Actividad Dos

Draw a line from the phrase in English to the phrase in Spanish. Then, draw a picture describing the phrase.

I swim

nado

you swim

I swim

nadas

you swim

Actividad Tres

Draw a line from the picture to the correct word in Spanish. Make sure to say the Spanish word out loud as you are drawing the line.

la pelota de playa

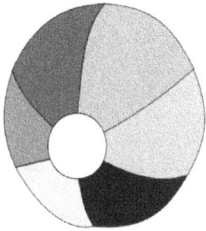

la concha

la playa

la arena

el mar

Actividad Cuatro

Counting Conchas

What you will need:

many *conchas* or a trip to the beach
bucket

What to do:

Option 1:

Take a trip to a beach. Pick up as many shells as you can find and put them in your bucket. Every time you pick one up, count it in Spanish.

Option 2:

Take all of the shells that you've collected before and give them to your parents. Let them hide the shells around your house or backyard. You can then search for the *conchas*. Every time you find a shell count it in Spanish.

Actividad Cinco

A Sandy Picture

What you will need:

a little sand
paper
markers, crayons or paint
glue stick

What to do:

1. Make your own beach picture.
2. Draw all of the items that are listed in this lesson (get your parent to help you if you need help.) As you draw each object, say its name in Spanish.
3. Color all of the items except the sand.
4. Rub the glue stick on the part of the picture that is sand.
5. Sprinkle sand on the glue and let dry.
6. Dust off remaining sand and hang up your picture. Every time you walk by your picture, point to the items and say their names in Spanish.

Lección 9
Race Cars

Vocabulary:

el coche de carrera
*ehl-**koh**-chay-day-kahr-**ray**-rah*
race car

la pista de carrera
*lah-**pee**-stah-day-kahr-**ray**-rah*
race track

la línea de salida
*lah-**lee**-nay-ah-day-sah-**lee**-dah*
starting line

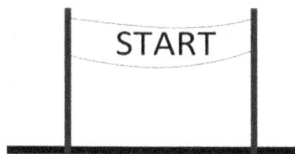

la carrera *lah-kahr-**ray**-rah*
race

la línea de meta
*lah-**lee**-nay-ah-day-**meh**-tah*
finish line

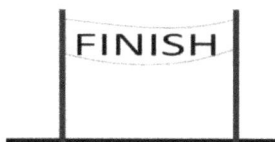

Fun Phrases:

gané	gah-**nay**	I won
ganaste	gah-**nah**-stay	you won
perdí	pehr-**dee**	I lost
perdiste	pehr-**dee**-stay	you lost

Challenge:

You can have your children remember the words for I won, you won, I lost, you lost, in Spanish or, if you feel they are ready for grammar, you can teach them a little about one of the past tenses of Spanish.

Spanish has a two different past tenses. The one that is introduced in this lesson is called preterite. Generally, it is used to describe an action that has been completed.

There are 3 classes of verbs in Spanish. They are based on their endings -ar, -er and -ir. I won - ganar is an -ar verb and I lost - perder is an -er verb.

To form the preterite tense take off the infinitive ending –ar, -er, or –ir and then add the preterite ending. -é for –ar verbs and -í for –er and –ir verbs for the first person singular (I). To conjugate for the second person singular (you), again take off the ending of the verb and then add –aste for –ar verbs and –iste for –er and –ir verbs.

ganar —> gan~~ar~~ —>gané (I won)

ganar —>gan~~ar~~ —>ganaste (you won)

perder —>perd~~er~~ —>perí (I lost)

perder —>perd~~er~~ —>periste (you lost)

Actividad Uno

 Look at the pictures of Ramón. Do you think he has won or lost in each picture? Circle the correct phrase that you think he is saying for each picture.

perdí	gané

perdí	gané

perdí	gané

Actividad Dos

Who won the race? Trace the lines to figure out who really won. Then, on the line at the bottom of the page, write the name of the person who won the race.

Claudia

Ramón

Pedro

_____ gané!

_____ won!

Actividad Tres

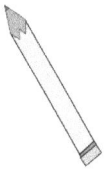

Ask your mom or dad to help you read these questions. Then, circle if you won or lost each one.

The last time you ran with a friend, did you win or lose?

Gané. Perdí.

The last board game you played with your parents, did you win or lose?

Gané. Perdí.

The last video game you played, did you win or lose?

Gané. Perdí.

The last contest you entered, did you win or lose?

Gané. Perdí.

Actividad Cuatro

Playing Games

What you will need:

any board or card game

What to do:

1. Play any board or card game that you have.
2. Try to use Spanish as much as you can during the game.
3. At the end of the game make sure you use your new phrases: *"Perdí."* and *"Gané"*.

Gané.

Actividad Cinco

A Speedy Car Race

What you will need:

toy cars
paper
masking tape

What to do:

1. Get your mom or dad to help you use masking tape on the carpet to make a race track (test a little area first to make sure that the tape doesn't damage the carpet).
2. Make a starting line and a finish line out of paper and put on the course.
3. Now it's time to start your engines!
4. Race your cars around and see which one wins. Make sure you use your Spanish as you play on your *pista de carrera*.

Lección 10
A Kingdom of Knights

Vocabulary:

el caballero
ehl-kah-bah-yay-roh
knight

el castillo
ehl-kahs-tee-yoh
castle

el rey
ehl-ray-ee
king

la reina
lah-ray-ee-nah
queen

Actividad Uno

Can you please help the knight get to the *castillo*? As you pass each person in the maze, say their name in Spanish.

Actividad Dos

Color this picture according to the color key below.

el caballero	azul y negro
el castillo	verde
la reina	amarillo
el rey	rojo y anaranjado

Actividad Tres

Fill in the missing letters and then draw a line from the picture to the correct Spanish word.

el ___e___

el cabal___ero

la re___n___a

Actividad Cuatro

Matching Game

You will need:
the matching cards from the back of this workbook
scissors

What to do:
1. Turn the cards upside-down.
2. Turn over two at a time to see if you have a pair of the picture and the correct word in Spanish.

Challenge:
Every time you make a match of cards, make a complete sentence with the word in Spanish! For example:

Como los dulces. - I eat the candies.

Actividad Cinco

Pulling it Together

You will need:
any toys or objects that you have for which you learned Spanish names in this workbook - stuffed sea animals, pirate hat, etc.
backpack

What to do:
1. Put all of the toys and objects in your backpack.
2. Surprise your parents or grandparents. Tell them you have something to show them.
3. Then, one by one, take out each object and say their names in Spanish. Try to make sentences too, if you would like to try.

Appendices

My Learning Slide

Every time you finish a *lección* in the book,
color a section of the learning slide.

Three cheers for

¡Felicidades!
Congratulations!
You have successfully finished
More Spanish for Little Boys.

1st

English to Spanish Dictionary

alien	el extraterrestre	*ehl-ex-trah-ter-**res**-tray*
basketball	el baloncesto	*ehl-bah-lohn-**sehs**-toh*
beach	la playa	*lah-**plah**-yah*
beach ball	la pelota de playa	*lah-pay-**loh**-tah-day-**plah**-yah*
bless you	salud	*sah-**lood***
cake	el pastel	*ehl-pahs-**tehl***
candy	los dulces	*lohs-**dool**-says*
castle	el castillo	*ehl-kahs-**tee**-yoh*
circus	el circo	*ehl-**seer**-koh*
clown	el payaso	*ehl-pah-**yah**-soh*
cookie	le galleta	*lah-gah-**yeh**-tah*
comet	la cometa	*lah-koh-**may**-tah*
cotton candy	el algodón dulce	*ehl-ahl-goh-**dohn**-**dool**-say*

crab	el cangrejo	*ehl-kan-**gray**-hoh*
cycling	el ciclismo	*ehl-see-**klees**-moh*
ear	la oreja	*lah-oh-**ray**-hah*
eighteen	dieciocho	*dee-ay-see-**oh**-choh*
eleven	once	***ohn**-say*
excuse me	perdón	*pehr-**dohn***
eye	el ojo	*ehl-**oh**-ho*
face	la cara	*lah-**kah**-rah*
finish line	la línea de meta	*lah-**lee**-nay-ah-day-**meh**-tah*
fifteen	quince	***keen**-say*
fourteen	catorce	*kah-**tohr**-say*
golf	el golf	*ehl-gohlf*
hair	el pelo	*ehl-**pay**-loh*
hat	el sombrero	*ehl-sohm-**bray**-roh*

English	Spanish	Pronunciation
have a good meal	buen apetito	*booehn-ah-pay-**tee**-toh*
ice hockey	el hockey sobre hielo	*ehl-**hoh**-kayee-**soh**-bray-ee-ay-loh*
I am scared	tengo miedo	***tayn**-goh-mee-**ay**-doh*
I am not scared	no tengo miedo	*noh-**tayn**-goh-mee-**ay**-doh*
I drink	bebo	***bay**-boh*
I eat	como	***koh**-moh*
I lost	perdí	*pehr-**dee***
I play	juego	*hoo-**ay**-goh*
I swim	nado	***nah**-doh*
I want	quiero	*kee-**eh**-roh*
I won	gané	*gah-**nay***
king	el rey	*ehl-**ray**-ee*
knight	el caballero	*ehl-kah-bah-**yay**-roh*

lion tamer	el domador de leones	*ehl-doh-mah-**dohr**-day-lee-**ohn**-ays*
lollypop	el pirulí	*ehl-pee-roo-**lee***
maybe	quizás	*kee-**sahs***
moon	la luna	*lah-**loo**-nah*
mouth	la boca	*lah-**boh**-kah*
no	no	*noh*
nose	la nariz	*lah-nah-**rees***
nice to meet you	mucho gusto	***moo**-choh-**goo**-stoh*
nineteen	diecinueve	*dee-ay-see-noo-**ay**-vay*
octopus	el pulpo	*ehl-**pool**-poh*
pirate	el pirata	*ehl-pee-**rah**-tah*
pirate ship	el barco pirata	*ehl-**bar**-koh-pee-**rah**-tah*
planet	el planeta	*ehl-plah-**nay**-tah*

queen	la reina	*lah-ray-**ee**-nah*
race	la carrera	*lah-kahr-**ray**-rah*
race car	el coche de carrera	*ehl-**koh**-chay-day -kahr-**ray**-rah*
race track	la pista de carrera	*lah-**pee**-stah-day- kahr-**ray**-rah*
ringmaster	el director de circo	*ehl-dee-rehk-**tohr** -day-**seer**-koh*
sand	la arena	*lah-ah-**ray**-nah*
sandcastle	el castillo de arena	*ehl-kah-**stee**-yoh- day-ah-**ray**-nah*
sea	el mar	*ehl-mahr*
seventeen	diecisiete	*dee-ay-see-see- **ay**-tay*
shark	el tiburón	*ehl-tee-boo-**rohn***
shell	la concha	*lah-**kohn**-chah*
sixteen	dieciséis	*dee-ay-see-**says***
soccer	el fútbol	*ehl-foot-**ball***
soda pop	el refresco	*ehl-ray-**frehs**-koh*

spaceship	la astronave	*lah-as-troh-**nah**-vay*
star	la estrella	*lah-ehs-**tray**-yah*
starfish	la estrella de mar	*lah-ehs-**tray**-yah-day-mahr*
starting line	la línea de salida	*lah-**lee**-nay-ah-day-sah-**lee**-dah*
sunglasses	las gafas de sol	*lahs-**gah**-fahs-day-sohl*
swimming	la natación	*lah-nah-tah-see-**ohn***
sword	la espada	*lah-ehs-**pah**-dah*
tight-rope walker	el funambulista	*ehl-foon-ah-boo-**lee**-stah*
thirteen	trece	***tray**-say*
treasure chest	el cofre del tesoro	*ehl-**koh**-fray-del-tay-**soh**-roh*
treasure map	el mapa del tesoro	*ehl-**mah**-pah-del-tay-**soh**-roh*
twelve	doce	***doh**-say*
twenty	veinte	***vayin**-tay*
very	muy	***moo**-ee*

whale	la ballena	*lah-bah-**yay**-nah*
yes	sí	*see*
you are not scared	no tienes miedo	*noh-tee-**ehn**-ehs-mee-**ay**-doh*
you are scared	tienes miedo	*tee-**ehn**-ehs-mee-**ay**-doh*
you drink	bebes	***bay**-behs*
you eat	comes	***koh**-mehs*
you lost	perdiste	*pehr-**dee**-stay*
you play	juegas	*hoo-**ay**-gahs*
you swim	nadas	***nah**-dahs*
you want	quieres	*kee-**eh**-rehs*
you won	ganaste	*gah-**nah**-stay*

Spanish to English Dictionary

el algodón dulce	*ehl-ahl-goh-**dohn-dool**-say*	cotton candy
la arena	*lah-ah-**ray**-nah*	sand
la astronave	*lah-as-troh-**nah**-vay*	spaceship
la ballena	*lah-bah-**yay**-nah*	whale
el baloncesto	*ehl-bah-lohn-**sehs**-toh*	basketball
el barco pirata	*ehl-**bar**-koh-pee-**rah**-tah*	pirate ship
bebes	***bay**-behs*	you drink
bebo	***bay**-boh*	I drink
la boca	*lah-**boh**-kah*	mouth
buen apetito	*booehn-ah-pay-**tee**-toh*	have a good meal
el caballero	*ehl-kah-bah-**yay**-roh*	knight

el castillo	*ehl-kahs-**tee**-yoh*	castle
el castillo de arena	*ehl-kah-**stee**-yoh-day-ah-**ray**-nah*	sandcastle
el cangrejo	*ehl-kan-**gray**-hoh*	crab
la cara	*lah-**kah**-rah*	face
la carrera	*lah-kahr-**ray**-rah*	race
catorce	*kah-**tohr**-say*	fourteen
el ciclismo	*ehl-see-**klees**-moh*	cycling
el circo	*ehl-**seer**-koh*	circus
el coche de carrera	*ehl-**koh**-chay-day-kahr-**ray**-rah*	race car
el cofre del tesoro	*ehl-**koh**-fray-del-tay-**soh**-roh*	treasure chest
comes	***koh**-mehs*	you eat
la cometa	*lah-koh-**may**-tah*	comet
como	***koh**-moh*	I eat

la concha	lah-**kohn**-chah	shell
diecinueve	dee-ay-see-noo-**ay**-vay	nineteen
dieciocho	dee-ay-see-**oh**-choh	eighteen
dieciséis	dee-ay-see-**says**	sixteen
diecisiete	dee-ay-see-see-**ay**-tay	seventeen
el director de circo	ehl-dee-rehk-**tohr**-day-**seer**-koh	ring master
el domador de leones	ehl-doh-mah-**dohr**-day-lee-**ohn**-ays	lion tamer
doce	**doh**-say	twelve
los dulces	lohs-**dool**-says	candy
la espada	lah-ehs-**pah**-dah	sword
la estrella	lah-ehs-**tray**-yah	star
la estrella de mar	lah-ehs-**tray**-yay-day-mahr	starfish
el extraterrestre	**ehl-ex-trah-ter-res-tray**	alien
el funambulista	ehl-foon-ah-boo-**lee**-stah	tight-rope walker

el fútbol	*ehl-**foot**-ball*	**soccer**
las gafas de sol	*lahs-**gah**-fahs-day-sohl*	***sunglasses***
le galleta	*lah-gah-**yeh**-tah*	***cookie***
ganaste	*gah-**nah**-stay*	**you won**
gané	*gah-**nay***	**I won**
el golf	*ehl-gohlf*	**golf**
el hockey sobre hielo	*ehl-**hoh**-kayee-**soh**-bray-ee-ay-loh*	**ice hockey**
juegas	*hoo-**ay**-gahs*	**you play**
juego	*hoo-**ay**-goh*	**I play**
la línea de meta	*lah-**lee**-nay-ah-day-**meh**-tah*	**finish line**
la línea de salida	*lah-**lee**-nay-ah-day-sah-**lee**-dah*	**starting line**
la luna	*lah-**loo**-nah*	**moon**
el mapa del tesoro	*ehl-**mah**-pah-del-tay-**soh**-roh*	**treasure map**

el mar	*ehl-mahr*	sea
mucho gusto	*moo-choh-goo-stoh*	nice to meet you
muy	*moo-ee*	very
nado	*nah-doh*	I swim
nadas	*nah-dahs*	you swim
la nariz	*lah-nah-rees*	nose
la natación	*lah-nah-tah-see-ohn*	swimming
no	*noh*	no
no tengo miedo	*noh-tayn-goh-mee-ay-doh*	I am not scared
el ojo	*ehl-oh-ho*	eye
once	*ohn-say*	eleven
la oreja	*lah-oh-ray-hah*	ear
el pastel	*ehl-pahs-tehl*	cake
el payaso	*ehl-pah-yah-soh*	clown

el pelo	*ehl-**pay**-loh*	hair
la pelota de playa	*lah-pay-**loh**-tah-day-**plah**-yah*	beach ball
perdí	*pehr-**dee***	I lost
perdiste	*pehr-**dee**-stay*	you lost
perdón	*pehr-**dohn***	excuse me
el pirata	*ehl-pee-**rah**-tah*	pirate
el pirulí	*ehl-pee-roo-**lee***	lollypop
el pista de carrera	*lah-**pee**-stah-day-kahr-**ray**-rah*	race track
el planeta	*ehl-plah-**nay**-tah*	planet
la playa	*lah-**plah**-yah*	beach
el pulpo	*ehl-**pool**-poh*	octopus
quieres	*kee-**eh**-rehs*	you want
quiero	*kee-**eh**-roh*	I want
quince	***keen**-say*	fifteen

quizás	*kee-**sahs***	maybe
el refresco	*ehl-ray-**frehs**-koh*	soda pop
la reina	*lah-ray-**ee**-nah*	queen
el rey	*ehl-**ray**-ee*	king
salud	*sah-**lood***	bless you
el sombrero	*ehl-sohm-**bray**-roh*	hat
tengo miedo	***tayn**-goh-mee-**ay**-do*	I am scared
trece	***tray**-say*	thirteen
el tiburón	*ehl-tee-boo-**rohn***	shark
tienes miedo	*tee-**ehn**-ehs-mee-**ay**-doh*	you are scared
veinte	***vayin**-tay*	twenty

Bingo

What you will need:
- Bingo cards – in this booklet.
- A hat or a cap.
- Something to cover up the squares on the cards, like dry beans or pennies.

What to do:
1. Cut out the cards on page 89, fold them and put them into a hat.
2. Draw one strip of paper out and say the word with the letter.
3. The children will cover up the word that they heard.
4. Repeat 4 and 5 until there is a winner!

B	I	N	G	O
		free square		

B	I	N	G	O
		free square		

B	I	N	G	O
		free square		

Cards for Bingo

B - el extraterrestre	B - la astronave	B - la cometa	B - la estrella	B - el barco pirata
B - el mapa del tesoro	B - el sombrero	B - el pirata	B - el cofre del tesoro	B - la espada
I - el extraterrestre	I - la astronave	I - la cometa	I - la estrella	I - el barco pirata
I - el mapa del tesoro	I - el sombrero	I - el pirata	I - el cofre del tesoro	I - la espada
N - el extraterrestre	N - la astronave	N - la cometa	N - la estrella	N - el barco pirata
N - el mapa del tesoro	N - el sombrero	N - el pirata	N - el cofre del tesoro	N - la espada
G - el extraterrestre	G - la astronave	G - la cometa	G - la estrella	G - el barco pirata
G - el mapa del tesoro	G - el sombrero	G - el pirata	G - el cofre del tesoro	G - la espada
O - el extraterrestre	O - la astronave	O - la cometa	O - la estrella	O - el barco pirata
O - el mapa del tesoro	O - el sombrero	O - el pirata	O - el cofre del tesoro	O - la espada

Matching Game

What to do:

1. Cut out the following cards. Paste them onto card   board for stability if you would like.
2. Turn the cards upside-down.
3. Turn over two at a time to see if you have a pair of the picture and the correct word in Spanish.

	la estrella de mar
	la cara
	la astronave

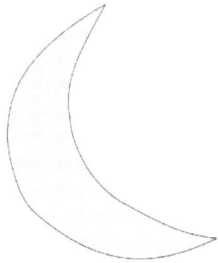

la luna

el pirata

el cofre del tesoro

el circo

	el fútbol
	los dulces
	el coche de carrera
	el caballero

www.ingramcontent.com/pod-product-compliance
Lightning Source LLC
Chambersburg PA
CBHW062106090426

42741CB00015B/3345